Essential Issues

WORLD

POPULATION

BY COURTNEY FARRELL

Content Consultant
Buffy Smith, PhD
associate professor of sociology and criminal justice
University of St. Thomas

ABDO
Publishing Company

CREDITS

Published by ABDO Publishing Company, 8000 West 78th Street, Edina, Minnesota 55439. Copyright © 2012 by Abdo Consulting Group, Inc. International copyrights reserved in all countries. No part of this book may be reproduced in any form without written permission from the publisher. The Essential Library™ is a trademark and logo of ABDO Publishing Company.

Printed in the United States of America,
North Mankato, Minnesota
062011
092011

 THIS BOOK CONTAINS AT LEAST 10% RECYCLED MATERIALS.

Editor: Karen Latchana Kenney
Copy Editor: Sarah Beckman
Interior Design and Production: Kazuko Collins
Cover Design: Marie Tupy

Library of Congress Cataloging-in-Publication Data
Farrell, Courtney.
  World population / by Courtney Farrell.
      p. cm. -- (Essential issues)
  Includes bibliographical references and index.
  ISBN 978-1-61783-138-6
  1. Population--Juvenile literature. 2. Overpopulation--Juvenile literature. I. Title.
  HB883.F37 2012
  304.6--dc22

                              2011009541

TABLE OF CONTENTS

A boy must wait to fill a container with water at a water depot in a slum of Delhi, India.

A Child in
a Crowded World

Nine-year-old Sandeep lives in a crowded slum on the outskirts of Delhi, India. In the morning, he emerges from his family's shack into a haze of smoke from hundreds of small coal-burning cooking fires.

Coal smoke stings the eyes and burns the throat. Chronic coughs are part of life in the slum, as is malnutrition. Almost 13 million people live in Delhi, and there is not enough food for them all. Dust coats Sandeep's stick-thin legs, but his appearance is not unusual. In India, half of all children are underweight.

Despite his hunger, Sandeep shares his morning milk with his dog before leaving for the day. He puts an arm protectively around his little brother as they walk out to the train tracks together. The boys are not taking a train to school, although they wish they could. Instead, they spend their days scavenging for bits of coal that fall from open-topped coal cars. It usually takes Sandeep most of a day to fill a sack with coal, since his brother is too small to help much. A bag of coal brings nine cents, enough money to buy some bread and a few vegetables. If Sandeep does not bring home coal to sell, his family will go hungry that evening.

Other kids play along the train tracks, but Sandeep does not join

Child Labor

Child labor does not refer to kids doing chores; it refers to the full-time employment of children. Child labor is illegal in India, as it is in most other nations, because unscrupulous employers can easily take advantage of child workers. It still continues in secret, though, especially in overpopulated countries where families are desperate for income.

Population Spikes

The population remained fairly stable until the eighteenth century, when the Industrial Revolution brought mechanization, increased use of fossil fuels, and improvements in medical care that allowed birth rates to increase. Ecologists who study populations of animals warn that such spikes in population are usually followed by equally sharp declines.

them. "I don't play here," he says. "I can't play; I have to work."[1] At nine years old, Sandeep is the sole supporter of his family. His mother has infants to tend to at home and his father is disabled. Since he was eight years old, Sandeep has supported them all.

When a train goes by, the boys look to see what it is carrying. If it is a coal train, Sandeep runs alongside and climbs aboard. Climbing on moving trains is incredibly dangerous. One slip can send a child down onto the track, to be crushed under the train's steel wheels. Sandeep knows the risk, but he cannot resist the chance to sweep armloads of coal off the coal car. He does it because his family needs the money.

OVERPOPULATION AFFECTS EVERYONE

How did Sandeep's family end up in such a bad situation? In short, the answer is overpopulation. Overpopulation occurs when a population grows too large for its resource base. A resource base includes everything that the land provides, such as crops,

In overpopulated areas, such as India, homelessness can be a major problem.

water, lumber, and minerals. Resources are always limited, especially when there are too many people using those resources. And when there are not enough resources for everyone, the result is poverty.

People try to solve the problem by growing more food and searching for more natural resources. Initially, these efforts pay off, but soon the expanding population needs even more. Settlements expand into less suitable areas, and wilderness goes under the plow. This expansion creates its own problems. When forests are felled to make room for farms, wild animals die or are killed by settlers. Tree roots no longer hold soil in place, and rain washes silt into rivers. Clean water becomes difficult to find as the quality of the environment declines. Communities suffer because the damaged land supports fewer people than it could before.

When populations grow too large, cities have trouble keeping up with the demands. Inhabitants may have trouble disposing of their waste, so pests, such as flies and rats, multiply. Stress, crowding, and poor hygiene increase the risk of disease. In extreme cases, food shortages can develop into famines. Competition for resources contributes to social inequality and even war. When a region is overpopulated, the quality of life declines for everyone, rich and poor alike.

War over Oil

Many of the armed conflicts in the world today are struggles over limited resources such as oil. Some people believe the war in Iraq was launched in 2003 to free the Iraqi people from the tyranny of Saddam Hussein, but Alan Greenspan, the eminent former head of the US Federal Reserve System, disagrees. "I am saddened that it is politically inconvenient to acknowledge what everyone knows: the Iraq war is largely about oil," Greenspan said.[2]

India Is Not Alone

India is by no means the only overpopulated nation. It serves as an example because it has already reached a crisis point. From 1965 to 1975, overcrowding and drought in India set off recurrent famines. Since then, education and economic diversification have made famines there unlikely, but the nation still suffers from the consequences of rapid population growth.

Approximately 25 percent of Indian citizens live in poverty. In large cities, families share apartments so small that residents have less space per person than they would in a US prison cell. Some residents of Bombay have no apartments at all; they sleep on sidewalks or in handmade mud and tin shelters. If the rest of the world's population continues to grow, more people will face the problems Indians face today.

The Pro-Population Growth Faction

Some people believe that overpopulation is a myth, arguing that open space still remains in places such as the western United States. Although it is true that the planet still has large tracts of unoccupied land, these places are empty for a reason. Generally, unoccupied places are too arid, windswept, or extreme in temperature to support settlements. Croplands there do not produce much, and little grass grows for livestock. Ecologists say such regions have low carrying capacities, which means that the land can support very few people or animals.

Population growth advocates see open rangeland and imagine that teeming cities of people could live there, but this is not true. Water is a limiting factor and sparsely populated places are likely to be that way because they are dry. Rivers support many cities, but even large rivers have their limits. So much water is tapped from the Colorado River that the river often runs dry before reaching the ocean. Groundwater is another source, but aquifers in the United States are nearing depletion. In recent years, the land around Phoenix, Arizona, has sunk as much as 18 feet (5 m) as aquifers beneath are pumped dry.

FINDING A SOLUTION

The Indian government has been trying for decades to control its nation's population explosion, but it has had little success. The birth rate has declined, but the population is still growing.

Overpopulation is a concern for the entire planet. Approximately 10 percent of the land on Earth is suitable for growing crops. Even if it were all used for food production, this finite planet would not be able to support infinite population growth.

The solution seems obvious: have fewer babies so that the human population can stabilize. This idea is simple to think about but very difficult to put into place. Many effective methods of birth control exist, but they are not always available. And some people choose not to use birth control or disagree with its use based on religious or personal beliefs.

The thorniest issue is the conflict between personal rights and the rights of society. Should a family be allowed to have as many children as they wish? Should a government be allowed to limit the number of children a woman can have? What will happen if humans do not learn to live sustainably on Earth? One issue is certain: humans are a part of nature, and they are subject to nature's limitations.

*Having a smaller family may be one part of
the solution to overpopulation.*

Reconstructions of what scientists believe human ancestors looked like are on display at the Museum of Natural History in New York.

THE STRUGGLE TO SURVIVE

O n this crowded planet, it is hard to imagine that humans have experienced times when they were close to extinction. Scientists know this through analysis of DNA, the molecule that encodes heritable information. In 1987, an exciting new discovery sprang out of scientific circles and into the mainstream media. DNA evidence showed conclusively that all humans today are descended from a single African female who lived 200,000 years ago.

The evidence came from mitochondrial DNA, a type of DNA that is inherited only through the mother. The idea was dubbed the "mitochondrial Eve" hypothesis, after the Biblical first woman. People everywhere marveled at the idea that all humans are really part of an extended family. Enthusiasm for the idea was so great that people of every race could be spotted wearing T-shirts proclaiming, "We are all Africans."

The fact that all humans came from a single ancestor does not mean that there were no other families living 200,000 years ago. Odds are that there were other families, but lineages ended when the last members of a family died out without leaving behind any surviving offspring. The mitochondrial Eve

Mitochondrial DNA

Microscopic structures called mitochondria are found within cells that provide the body with energy. Interestingly, mitochondria are descended from free-living bacteria that found their way inside ancestral cells and survived there. Because of this, they have their own DNA. All of the mitochondria a person has came from his or her mother, since the person is descended from the mitochondria of the mother's ovum, or egg. Sperm cells have mitochondria too, but those mitochondria die after the sperm cells leave a man's body.

hypothesis suggests that the human population went through a bottleneck—an event that caused a decrease in the population. The climate in Africa was becoming colder and drier around this time, but there is no proof that this caused a die-off. It could have been an epidemic disease, a natural disaster, or another culprit yet to be discovered.

The Toba Catastrophe Theory

Genetic studies across the globe have returned some interesting results. It turns out that people, despite their vast numbers, are not very genetically diverse. Racial differences are superficial, indicating that they evolved relatively recently. Under the skin, humans are a homogeneous lot.

"We share a common genetic ancestry that far outweighs physical differences—99.9 percent of all DNA is the same," explained Nayan Chanda of the Yale Center for the Study of Globalization.[1]

This lack of genetic diversity reveals that early people must have survived a second bottleneck, probably between 50,000 and 100,000 years ago. A massive volcanic eruption occurred 71,000 years ago on the island of Sumatra, in modern-day Indonesia. The eruption was the biggest in 25 million years, and ash from it spread north across India in deposits three to 20 feet (1 to 6 m) thick. The eruption was so huge that it left a 62-mile- (100-km-) long crater, which became Toba Lake.

University of Illinois professor Stanley H. Ambrose believes that the Toba eruption killed off most of the human race, leaving as few as 15,000 scattered survivors. Although not all experts are convinced, the timing of the eruption coincides well with geneticists' estimate of the date of the second bottleneck.

The Molecular Clock

Scientists use a technique called the molecular clock to determine when two populations last had a common ancestor. Mutations, or random changes in DNA, occur at a fairly constant rate. Therefore, groups that were separated a long time ago should have more differences between them today than groups that diverged recently. The technique can be used to map human migrations, such as the movement of early people out of Africa.

A Volcanic Winter

More devastating than the Toba eruption would have been the volcanic winter that followed it. Ash and sulfur dioxide from the eruption became suspended in the atmosphere. They reflected sunlight, creating a winter that lasted six years. An ice age followed that lasted 1,000 years. Countless individuals who survived the volcanic eruption could have perished later of cold and hunger. Tropical regions would have provided the best refuges.

According to the Toba Catastrophe Theory, small groups of survivors migrated out of the tropics and repopulated the world. The theory is not universally accepted, but if it turns out to be true, it would explain why the human race has so little genetic diversity.

"When our African recent ancestors passed through the prism of Toba's volcanic winter, a rainbow of differences appeared," Professor Ambrose said, referring to racial differences that he thinks evolved as isolated groups of survivors adapted to their surroundings.[2]

HUNTER-GATHERERS

The survivors of the two bottleneck events continued to live as hunter-gatherers until 7,000 to 10,000 years ago. Hunter-gatherers did not grow their own food, but foraged for wild plants and animals. Anthropological studies of contemporary hunter-gatherer societies provide a glimpse into the lives of ancestral humans. If early humans lived similarly to contemporary hunter-gatherers, they had gender-based divisions of labor. The men hunted large game, and women gathered plant foods. Most groups were probably small, made of

Modern hunter-gatherers, such as the Basarwa tribe of Botswana, exist in small numbers in remote places around the world.

just a few families. They were usually nomadic, except in the most abundant environments. In less productive places, tribes moved regularly in pursuit of wild game and edible plants.

Modern people may imagine this to be a grueling lifestyle, with every moment spent in a desperate search for food. The seventeenth-century philosopher Thomas Hobbes influenced this perception with his famous description of life "in the state of nature" as "solitary, poor, nasty, brutish, and short."[3] In fact, contemporary hunter-gatherers have more free time than urban dwellers do. Even in challenging environments such as the Kalahari Desert of Africa, indigenous Kung hunter-gatherers find all the food they need for the day in three or four hours. Tribes in more productive environments forage for just over an hour a day. The rest of the time they relax, create art, and socialize.

FEMALE FERTILITY

Groups of hunter-gatherers tended to naturally maintain low population densities, so they rarely exceeded the carrying capacity of the land. The physiological basis for this is based on the activity level of the women and the quality of the food the women ate. Female gatherers ate a high-vitamin, low-calorie diet, and exercised daily. As a result, most of them had very little body fat.

The Ages of Human History

Human history is divided into ages based on the tools that were in use at each time period. During the Stone Age, people had not yet learned to use metals. Tools were made not only of stone, but also wood, bone, and hide. The Stone Age is divided into three periods: the early (Paleolithic), middle (Mesolithic), and late (Neolithic). The Stone Age was followed by the Bronze Age, which was followed by the Iron Age. No exact dates correspond to these ages because societies around the globe developed at different rates.

In general, a thin adolescent girl will not begin to menstruate until she builds up a sufficient reserve of body fat to sustain a pregnancy and subsequent breastfeeding. This happens because adipose tissue (body tissue that stores fat) produces the female hormone estrogen. Late maturation means fewer total babies per woman. However, it is only part of the reason that hunter-gatherers did not overpopulate their environments.

Another factor that reduced the birth rate among hunter-gatherers is that mothers normally stop ovulating for a few months after the birth of a baby. This period of infertility is extended by breastfeeding. Mothers in those primitive societies may have breastfed their children for up to five years. This natural factor helped to space the birth of babies from two to four years apart.

The final factor that kept early humans in balance with their environment was the fact that they could not store large amounts of food. If a drought struck, or a population grew too large for its land base, the surplus population would starve. It was brutal, but it maintained the balance of nature. By living as hunter-gatherers, humans existed for thousands of years in relatively stable numbers.

THE NEOLITHIC REVOLUTION

The Neolithic Revolution was the transition from a hunter-gatherer lifestyle to farming. This shift occurred independently in different parts of the world and among different cultures. One of the first peoples to settle in one place were the Natufians of the Middle East, whose members began building permanent homes approximately 14,000 years ago. During this time period, the last Ice Age was ending. The land in the Middle East was not as arid as it is today; much of it was fertile and forested. Grains grew wild in the meadows, and people learned to cultivate and store them. The transition from a nomadic to a settled lifestyle did not occur quickly. But by 7,000 years ago, the majority of people in the Middle East lived in villages. The Neolithic Revolution spread slowly. It reached the British Isles for the first time in 4,500 BCE, some 5,000 years after it began.

The new settled lifestyle triggered an increase in population. Carbohydrate-rich farm foods were high in calories, allowing females to reach sexual maturity rapidly and produce babies in rapid succession. This was a welcome development to farm families, who wanted many children to help with the work. Many hands were needed to raise and harvest crops and guard the flocks.

Along with new farming skills and the domestication of animals, came new careers. Since one farmer could feed more than one person, not everyone had to farm. Others were free to learn specialized skills and become artisans or merchants. A warrior class was needed to defend storehouses of food against raiders. Societies began developing hierarchies, with politicians and warriors at the top. Civilization was underway.

Why Switch to Farming?

Neolithic farmers must have lived difficult lives. Excavations of early farming settlements revealed that the first farmers were not very healthy people. Their skeletons were stunted, and they showed signs of nutritional deficiencies. Neolithic people knew nothing about nutrition, and they probably subsisted largely on a few crops. Many died young, with teeth decaying from their carbohydrate-rich diets. In contrast, hunter-gatherer skeletons revealed that they had been tall, strong, and healthy. So why did Neolithic people choose to farm at all?

UCLA professor Dr. Jared Diamond believes that farming may have provided a more certain return than foraging. That is certainly possible if wild foods were being depleted. Early hunters have been implicated in the extinction of large animals toward the end of the Pleistocene (10,000 years ago). Perhaps wild edible plants were becoming scarce as well.

Another possibility is that it was a learned behavior. Children learn life skills from their parents, so children of farmers became farmers. Sedentary populations have higher birth rates, so perhaps, as Professor Diamond suggested, "those groups of hunter-gatherers who adopted food production outbred those who didn't."[4]

Until recent decades, scholars viewed the advent of civilization with undisguised pride, acknowledging none of its negative repercussions. Current thinkers tend to take a more objective approach. As Professor Diamond put it:

> *However great the achievement of the Neolithic Revolution, it must be noted that this point in history marks the beginning of the growth of the human population. Of course, overpopulation was not an issue thousands of years ago. The population would not spike until the Industrial Revolution, but the root of the population problem can be traced all the way back to the introduction of farming.*[5]

Primitive Living Schools

Students who are interested in the Neolithic period can spend a few weeks at a primitive-living skills camp. Counselors there teach Stone Age skills, such as flint knapping (shaping a stone into a rough tool), kayak making, and wilderness survival. The camps are fun and educational for students, who learn to appreciate the strength and creativity of their ancestors.

It is not an option for 6.8 billion humans to return to a hunter-gatherer lifestyle, nor would many people choose that lifestyle. Children from indigenous cultures spent years learning all the skills they needed to live off the land. Much of that knowledge is lost now. There is no turning back. The solution must be found by moving forward, or not at all.

The Neolithic period marked a transition from a hunting-gathering lifestyle to a settled lifestyle.

*The unclean conditions of medieval towns made
their citizens vulnerable to disease.*

INFLUENCES ON
POPULATIONS

Throughout history, disease has been one
of the most important limiting factors
on human populations. When people lived in
scattered bands, diseases that struck one tribe
did not spread easily to others. As populations

increased, the risk of disease rose as well. During the Middle Ages (476 to 1453) towns began to grow. Hygiene was poor, mostly because towns did not have effective systems of sewage disposal. Residents used chamber pots as toilets and simply emptied them into the streets. Fleas and rats multiplied, and epidemics raged across the land.

EPIDEMICS KILLED MILLIONS

The first epidemic to devastate Europe was the Plague of Justinian, which was named after the leader of the Byzantine Empire where the outbreak began. During Justinian's reign, his empire already held more people than the land could support. Grain was imported from Egypt to feed the people. In 540, a plague arrived on one of the grain ships. As grain was transported along trade routes, the disease traveled with it. The Plague of Justinian did not end

Limiting Factors

The factors that limit population growth are grouped into two categories: density-dependent and density-independent. Density-dependent factors are those that worsen with crowding, such as war, disease, and competition for food. Density-independent factors include events that are potentially lethal whether an area is overpopulated or not. Examples of density-independent limits on population growth include natural disasters such as droughts, volcanic eruptions, or hurricanes.

until the year 590, 50 years later. By then, half of Europe's population lay dead.

The Plague of Justinian occurred so long ago that historians are not certain of the organism that caused it. It was probably the bacterium *Yersinia pestis*, the causative agent of the disease known as plague or the Black Plague. The plague may have started because a shipment of Egyptian grain carried stowaways— mice that were hiding in the grain. On those mice were plague-infected fleas. When their rodent host died, the fleas would hop

The Plague Today

The plague bacterium *Yersinia pestis* is still alive in the world today, carried by some squirrels, prairie dogs, rabbits, and rats. In the United States, plague is found in Arizona, New Mexico, Colorado, California, Nevada, and Oregon. Animals in Africa, Asia, and South America also carry it. The organism is susceptible to antibiotics. But in recent decades, outbreaks have occurred in India and Africa.

Isolated cases in the United States occur when a person is bitten by an infected flea living on a wild rodent. In 1992, an Arizona man died when he was infected by a flea on his cat, which had been hunting chipmunks. To avoid possible exposure, people should not handle wild rodents that appear ill or disoriented.

Symptoms of plague are different, depending on which type of the disease is involved. Bubonic plague is named for the buboes, or swollen lymph nodes that appear on the neck, groin, or armpits. Pneumonic plague, contracted by inhalation of cough droplets, is characterized by a cough with bloody sputum, high fever, and vomiting. The last type of plague is septicemia, an infection of the bloodstream. This type of plague gave the disease its medieval names, the Black Plague or the Black Death, because it blackens a victim's extremities.

off and look for another host to bite. Once a person was bitten by a plague-infected flea and became infected, the disease could be rapidly transmitted from person to person.

The Black Plague

Plague returned to Europe in 1347 and remained at its height until 1352. During this time, it was known as the Black Plague. The infected fleas were carried on rats instead of mice, but medieval people did not know this. Many believed that the epidemic was God's punishment for their sins. Approximately 25 million people, or one-third of the population of Europe, died. So many deaths occurred over so short a period that the survivors were overwhelmed by the amount of bodies that amassed.

"Although the cemeteries were full they were forced to dig huge trenches, where they buried the bodies by hundreds. Here they stowed them away like bales in the hold of a ship and covered them with a little earth, until the whole trench was full," wrote Giovanni Boccaccio, who witnessed the plague in the Italian city of Florence in 1348.[1]

Other epidemics would come and go, but the Black Plague was the last event to cause a noticeable

Foundries, such as the Peel and Williams Foundry in Manchester, England, flourished during the Industrial Revolution.

decline in the graph of the human population. Following the recovery from that ordeal, the number of people on Earth slowly began to increase again.

THE EUROPEAN INDUSTRIAL REVOLUTION

The population curve really began to spike during the Industrial Revolution. This was a period of technological innovation and social change that began in England around 1770. It was marked by an increasing reliance on fossil fuels, especially coal. The steam engine was invented, along with the first machines for spinning and weaving. Although these advancements seem like positive developments, they brought a great deal of human suffering with them. Cloth making had been a cottage industry, but it became centralized into large, oppressive factories that are remembered for their exploitation of child workers. Society was unprepared for the onslaught of births, and poverty was rife.

Though the Industrial Revolution wound down around 1900, scholars still do not fully understand its effect on the population. Ecologists theorize that the boosted food production resulting from the use of fossil fuels brought on a population explosion. However, advances in medicine and hygiene were influential as well.

Which event provided the driving force for the baby boom? Did population pressure stimulate innovation? Or did innovation increase the food supply, so more

The General Enclosure Act of 1845

The General Enclosure Act of 1845 forced English peasants off the land so that aristocratic landowners could improve their estates. This meant that instead of allowing various tenants to farm strips of land in their own way, entire estates were managed professionally. Wealthy landowners took an interest in modernized farming techniques, and livestock breeding became a science. These advancements increased food production at a time when impoverished peasants were flooding into cities looking for work.

people survived? The larger food supply probably came first, but this would be difficult to prove. In either case, by the 1800s, the population became enough of a concern to be an issue for debate.

The Industrial Revolution Continues

The term *Industrial Revolution* usually refers to industrial development in Europe from 1770 to 1900. However, it should be noted that other nations underwent (or are currently undergoing) their own industrial revolutions on separate timelines. An industrial revolution happens when a country's industry changes from operating by means of manual labor or animal power to mechanized systems.

THOMAS MALTHUS AND HIS POPULATION ESSAYS

One of the first authors to address the population issue was the British scholar Thomas Robert Malthus, who lived from 1766 to 1834. Malthus proposed the idea that the capacity of populations to reproduce could exceed the ability of the land to support them. In 1803, Malthus wrote:

Through the animal and vegetable kingdoms, nature has scattered the seeds of life abroad with the most profuse and liberal hand. She has been comparatively sparing in the room, and the nourishment necessary to rear them . . . The race of plants, and race of animals shrink under this great restrictive law. And the race of man cannot, by any efforts of reason, escape from it. Among plants and animals its effects are waste of seed, sickness, and premature death. Among mankind, misery and vice.[2]

In Malthus's view, "misery and vice" came in the form of disease, famine, and war. Malthus's essays were controversial because he argued that benevolent acts, such as feeding the poor or curing disease, exacerbated overpopulation. In this way, he believed, charity ultimately worsened the suffering it attempted to alleviate.

If the population continued to grow unchecked, Malthus predicted a world in which "epidemics, pestilence, and plagues advance in terrific array. . . . Should success be still incomplete, gigantic inevitable famine stalks in the rear, and with one mighty blow levels the population."[3]

Some opposed Malthus's population outlook, though. William

Charles Darwin

The ideas of Thomas Malthus influenced Charles Darwin, the author of *The Origin of Species*. In this book, Darwin explains his theory of evolution by natural selection. In 1838, Darwin read Malthus's essays and noticed that although populations do have the ability to overgrow their environments, most do not do so. This led to his observation that there is a struggle for survival, and individuals who are best adapted to their environment have the most offspring. Over time, the entire population resembles the successful individuals, and evolution has occurred.

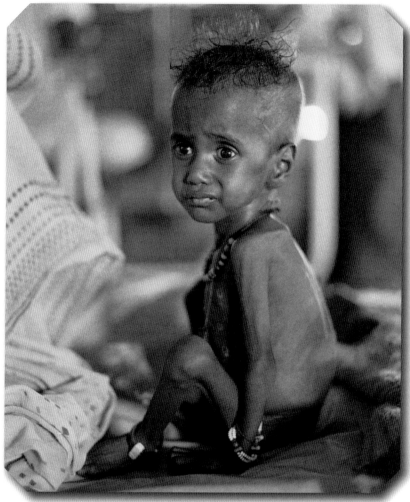

Starvation in underdeveloped countries encouraged scientists to engineer new and more productive ways to grow food.

Godwin, the father of *Frankenstein* author Mary Shelley, was one of those in opposition. Godwin, like many aristocratic Britons of the time, believed that technological progress would eventually solve all of society's problems. This debate continues essentially unchanged today.

THE GREEN REVOLUTION

By the 1960s, populations in some regions were beginning to exceed local carrying capacities. Televised images in the 1980s of starving children in China, Africa, and South Asia shocked Western audiences. US agricultural scientists went to work, scouring the globe for productive varieties of grains. Research stations crossbred strains and selected the winners. The seeds, along with fertilizers and chemicals needed to grow them, were distributed around the world. Technology brought bumper harvests to the rescue, just as William Godwin had envisioned. The Green Revolution was a historical event. For the first time, a species had intentionally increased the carrying capacity of the planet.

India was the greatest success story of the Green Revolution. In 1950, its grain production of 50.8 megatons (46 million metric tons) was not quite enough to feed its population of 361 million people. New strains of grain, along with chemical fertilizers and pesticides, brought the total to

82 megatons (74 million metric tons) by 1960. The world celebrated, believing the starving multitudes to be saved. But there was a hitch; by 1960, the Indian population was up to 439 million.

Decade by decade, researchers raced to keep production ahead of population. By 1970, 108 megatons (98 million metric tons) of grain had to feed 548 million Indians. The land and water were affected with chemical fertilizers, pesticides, and herbicides in a desperate bid to squeeze more calories from every acre. By the year 2000, India was producing a whopping 201.8 megatons (183 million metric tons) of grain. As a result, however, its population had reached 1 billion.

*Thomas Malthus believed that famine was inescapable
in an overpopulated world.*

Crowded housing is typical in Indian cities.

PREDICTING THE FUTURE

As of 2010, there were roughly 6,884,215,263 people on Earth and 363,554 more are born every day. Approximately 154,138 people die every day. The total change in population is measured by subtracting the number of deaths from the number of births. Using this calculation, the US Census Bureau determined that the world's population is increasing by approximately 209,416 people each day.

In a startling analogy, population expert George D. Moffett described this trend as being equivalent to adding "a new Pittsburgh or Boston every two days, a new Germany every eight months, a new Mexico or two new Canadas every year."[1]

Populations grow so fast because they increase exponentially. An example of an exponential increase is this sequence: 2, 4, 8, 16, 32, 64. Careful examination of these numbers reveals that they are not only increasing; they are increasing at an increasing rate. In other words, the rate of exponential population growth speeds up over time, so each jump is larger than the one before.

Moffett explained this idea in terms of human history, saying, "It took eighteen centuries from the time of Christ for the earth to reach its first one billion inhabitants but only one century to reach its second and only one decade to reach its latest billion."[2]

These trends cannot continue forever. After a period of exponential growth, natural populations always stabilize or decline. Technology has enabled humans to delay this stabilization, but not prevent it.

THREE SCENARIOS FOR 2050

In 2002, the United Nations (UN) created three population projections for the year 2050, based on high, medium, or low reproductive rates. The high-growth scenario was calculated by estimating the current rate of growth into the future. This means if birth and death rates remain unchanged, there will be 10.6 billion people on the planet by the year 2050.

Population Estimates and Projections

The UN population projections illustrate the long-term results of current trends, but they do not predict the future. The high-growth model increases infinitely, while the low-growth model declines to an implied extinction of humanity. It is important to note that scientists are not predicting either infinite growth or the extinction of the human race.

The medium-growth prediction is the one that most experts think is likely. This model puts the population in 2050 at 8.9 billion, which is an increase of 47 percent from the year 2000. Of this population growth, 99 percent is expected to occur in developing nations. A developing nation is a country that is not highly industrialized and generally poorer than developed nations.

The low-growth model still shows a substantial population increase, to 7.4 billion. In this scenario, population will continue to increase until approximately 2030, slowly level off, and then decline to less than 4 billion by 2150. In order to achieve this outcome, worldwide fertility would need to drop below the replacement level of 2.1 children per family. This is already occurring in Europe, where many families have a single child.

LONG-TERM PROJECTIONS

The UN's population projections go to the year 2300, but the value of the numbers is disputed. The high-growth model predicts a world population that reaches 36.4 billion by 2300 and continues to increase.

The high-growth model is mathematically correct in the sense that 6.5 billion people increasing at the current rate of 0.25 percent annually comes to 36.4 billion in approximately 300 years. However, this model is unrealistic, not only because it is doubtful that the planet

Two-Child Families

The family size needed to keep the population stable is 2.1 children per woman. The one-tenth increase over two (from two children born to replace every two parents) comes from the fact that not all babies born will survive to adulthood. As of 2010, women in developing countries bore an average of 3.11 children each, but this number is predicted to fall to 2.04 by 2050.

could support 36 billion people, but also because it predicts never-ending growth.

Global Extremes in Life Expectancies

Life expectancy is the average life span of a person from a particular population. This statistic is a benchmark for the overall health of a nation or area, with higher life expectancies reflecting better nutrition and health care. Generally, life expectancies are higher for developed nations than for developing ones. However, high rates of childhood obesity in the United States are expected to result in the first ever decline in that nation's life expectancy. As of 2010, the five nations with the highest life expectancies were:

- Monaco: 89.78 years
- Macau: 84.38 years
- San Marino: 82.95 years
- Andorra: 82.36 years
- Japan: 82.17 years

Low life expectancies in developing nations should not be interpreted as the oldest age residents achieve. The statistic is an average. If a country has high childhood mortality rates, it drives down the life expectancy number. Even in a nation with a low life expectancy, some individuals will reach advanced ages. As of 2010, the five nations with the lowest life expectancies were:

- Angola: 38.48 years
- Mozambique: 41.37 years
- Afghanistan: 44.65 years
- Nigeria: 47.24 years
- Zimbabwe: 47.55 years

LIFE EXPECTANCY

The UN predicts that, over time, life expectancy will increase almost everywhere in the world. From 1950 to 2000, global life expectancy increased by 20 years. It should go up another ten years by 2050, giving the average human a life expectancy of 76 years. For comparison, in 2010, life expectancy was 68.9 years globally and 78.2 years in the United States. An exception to this trend is Africa, where the HIV/AIDS epidemic has already caused life expectancy to decline by an average of 11 years.

Age Structure Diagrams

Age structure diagrams are graphs that tell the reader at a glance if a population is growing or not. These diagrams display the percentages of males and females of each age in a population, showing the proportions that are pre-reproductive (infancy to 14), reproductive (15 to 44), or post-reproductive (45 and up). Developed nations with stable populations have age structure diagrams that would be evenly shaped.

Age structure diagrams of developing nations, such as Kenya, Nigeria, and Saudi Arabia, have a wide pyramid shape, which indicates that a large proportion of the population is young. The United States, Australia, Canada, and China have age structures shaped like cones. This shows that they are growing slowly.

Nations such as Austria, Denmark, and Italy have the reverse trend. Their populations are slowly declining, so age structure diagrams for these

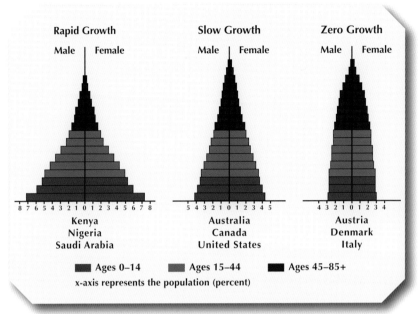

Three types of growth are shown on an age structure diagram: rapid growth, slow growth, and zero growth.

nations are narrower at the base than the other growth models. Declining populations are good news for nature, but they strain societies. These countries have relatively few young people to bear the burden of supporting a large number of seniors.

DEMOGRAPHIC TRANSITION

Demographers (scientists who study populations) theorize that nations pass through four stages of development. Stage I, the preindustrial stage, is characterized by high birth and death rates, resulting in slow overall population growth. Stage 2, the transitional stage, occurs when vaccinations and improved health care result in lower death rates in developing nations. Initially, transitional countries retain their high birth rates, so population increases rapidly. By stage 3, the industrial stage, birth and death rates have both declined, and the population is growing slowly. Stage 4, the postindustrial stage, is the hallmark of a healthy, successful society. Birth and death rates are low, so the population stabilizes.

Factors such as large national debts, lack of industrialization, high rates of disease, and a shortage of scientists and engineers can slow demographic transitions in developing countries. In a trend dubbed "brain drain," educated young people from developing

Age Structure Diagrams

A pyramidal age structure predicts rapid population growth in the near future, because many young people will reach reproductive age at once. A conical age structure is characteristic of a slowly growing population. A rectangular age structure, pointed only at the top, means that most babies survive to adulthood and that most adults survive to become elderly.

nations often immigrate to developed countries. While this is a positive choice for those individuals, it is a loss for their native lands.

Age structure diagrams predict an increase in world population, but how far will it go? Will the UN's medium-growth scenario come true? Or will resource shortages and environmental damage stop population growth in its tracks? ⌐

It is difficult to predict how large the population will grow on Earth.

When bees pollinate flowers, they are providing an ecosystem service.

ECOSYSTEM SERVICES

Behind the scenes, the planet functions to provide the conditions needed for people to survive. Plants produce oxygen, bees pollinate crops, and microbes degrade waste. These are examples of ecosystem services—resources and processes provided by nature. Some ecosystem services are easy to recognize, such as timber, fiber, food, or fuel. Others go unnoticed. After all, who pays attention when the ocean absorbs carbon dioxide from the atmosphere? And when the ozone layer stops ultraviolet radiation from reaching Earth, it happens high in the atmosphere and out of sight.

Man-Made Natural Disaster

People tend to ignore ecosystem services until those services stop functioning. This happened in Guatemala, where old-growth forests absorbed rainwater from tropical storms. In mountainous areas, tree roots held hillsides in place, but no one noticed this until the trees were gone. In the twentieth century, logging companies arrived in search of mahogany, which is a hardwood that sells for as much as $35 per cubic foot ($1,600/cu m). Villagers also cut trees for firewood and to clear land for growing herds of livestock.

By September 6, 2010, too much of the forest was gone for it to perform its function. Raindrops were no longer caught softly in foliage, and storms pounded the bare slopes until they gave way. In the village of Nahuala, a tremendous mudslide came down on a road, burying a bus and other vehicles. Rescuers trying to dig them out were engulfed by a second mudslide, and 45 people died.

"My son, he was working with me—he was helping, out of solidarity," said a surviving rescuer. "He was scraping the earth to the side with a hoe, I was with the shovel . . . but I lost him and I can't do anything about it."[1]

After the disaster, Byron Pivaral, director of the government agency that manages road construction, said that widespread

The Hole in the Ozone Layer

Ozone (O_3) is a molecule containing three oxygen atoms. The ozone layer floats high in the atmosphere, approximately six to 30 miles (10 to 48 km) above the ground. There, it performs an invaluable function, blocking 97 to 99 percent of the ultraviolet (UV) radiation from the sun. This is an essential ecosystem service because one kind of UV radiation, UVB, causes sunburns and increases the risk of cataracts and skin cancer.

Ozone is valuable in the upper atmosphere, but at ground level, it is a pollutant. It is corrosive and irritating to the respiratory tract, and it can damage crops. Ozone is created naturally in the high atmosphere, but low-altitude ozone is created when automobile exhaust reacts with oxygen.

Man-made chemicals including chlorofluorocarbons (CFCs) react with O_3 and destroy it. CFCs were used as coolants for refrigerators, as propellants in aerosol cans, and for cleaning electronic devices. CFCs and other ozone-destroying chemicals are being phased out, so their use will be increasingly restricted until substitutes are found.

In the early 1980s, scientists began to detect a thinning of the ozone layer over Antarctica. This "hole" in the ozone layer is a special concern for residents of New Zealand, Australia, and Argentina, who are getting increased doses of UV radiation.

deforestation made it difficult for the land around the highway to absorb heavy rain. Hungry villagers had cut the trees beside the highway in order to plant corn and beans.

Watershed management is an ecosystem service. When environmental destruction disrupts it, either floods or drought may result.

FORESTS CREATE RAIN

The idea that forests make rain seems counterintuitive. After all, trees pull water out of the ground, so this would seem to dry out the land. Trees do increase rainfall, though, because water moves up through their roots and evaporates from their leaves in a process called transpiration. Water also evaporates directly off stems and tree trunks. This moisture returns to the land as precipitation.

Climatologist Roni Avissar, dean of the Rosenstiel School of Marine and Atmospheric Science, researched the effect of Amazon rainfall on global climate. He discovered that

Protecting Watersheds

Watersheds are areas of land defined by the drainage of water. All the precipitation that falls into one watershed drains to the same place. Individuals can help protect their watersheds by not using bug sprays or weed killers in their yards. When it rains, these poisons run off and fall into storm drains, which connect directly to rivers. Rivers fill the reservoirs that provide drinking water for local communities.

On October 4, 2005, Hurricane Stan slammed into Central America. Two thousand people died in Guatemala, mostly due to mudslides and flooding. The storm caused damage to Guatemalan roads, bridges, and crops, with the worst damage occurring in deforested areas. Climatologists warn that global warming-related increases to sea-surface temperature will continue to boost the power of hurricanes.

half the rain that falls on the Amazon rainforest evaporates, sending warm, moist air north to the United States and south to Argentina. Large man-made clearings of more than 62 miles (100 km) across in the rainforest disrupt this process. With a massive loss of trees, a forest cannot sustain its humidity. The number of thunderstorms with rainfall drops dramatically. This leads to a loss of rainfall in the rainforest as well as in other countries.

Americans might think that mudslides in Guatemala are only a problem for Guatemalans. Actually, these mudslides are symptoms of a problem that could affect the United States too. If enough rainforest is destroyed, floods could increase in the tropics, while rainfall on US farms could decline. This makes agriculture in the United States dependent on the survival of the rainforest.

Climate Change

Studying environmental problems is like pulling on a tangled string; every knot turns out to be

Melting polar ice is thought to be a result of climate change.

connected to all the others. This is because ecological processes on Earth are all interconnected, so destruction in one place has repercussions elsewhere. Some of the repercussions of deforestation are extinction of species, loss of medicinal plants, and the destruction of indigenous societies.

Another repercussion of deforestation is climate change. Climate change is also known as global warming because most regions of the planet are heating up. Polar ice caps are melting, and experts are concerned that sea levels could rise high enough to threaten coastal communities. Most scientists agree that greenhouse gases, which are gases that trap heat in the atmosphere, cause global warming. Carbon dioxide is a key greenhouse gas that comes from the combustion of fossil fuels. It is also released when forests are destroyed. Trees and plants help maintain a healthy atmospheric balance by storing carbon dioxide in their leaves, wood, roots, and the soil. When forests are destroyed, the stored carbon dioxide is released. Deforestation contributes 25 percent of the global emissions of carbon dioxide.

Charles, the Prince of Wales, believes deforestation to be an important issue, saying:

Greenhouse Gases

The top four greenhouse gases include:
1. Water vapor: from evaporation of bodies of water
2. Carbon dioxide: from respiration and burning of fossil fuels
3. Methane: from bacterial metabolism and melting of permafrost
4. Nitrous oxide: from animal manure, sewage treatment plants, and the combustion of fossil fuels

The world's forests need to be seen for what they are: giant global utilities, providing essential services to humanity on a vast scale. Rainforests store carbon, which is lost to the atmosphere when they burn, increasing global warming. The life they support cleans the atmosphere of pollutants and feeds it with moisture. They help regulate our climate and sustain the lives of some of the poorest people on this Earth. [2]

THE CURRENT MASS EXTINCTION

Humans are straining the world's resources to the limit. Deforestation and climate change are only two of the problems the planet faces today. Pollution, depleted fisheries, and declining freshwater supplies are concerns as well. Irrigation water for farms is growing scarce, raising concerns about future food security. The root cause of all those problems is overpopulation.

However, overpopulation is not just a problem for people. It is a catastrophe for other species—species that are disappearing in the greatest mass extinction since the passing of the dinosaurs. Geologic records show that there have been five mass extinctions in the history of the planet. The most recent one, 65 million years ago, happened when a giant asteroid slammed into Earth, igniting firestorms across the globe. Dinosaurs, along with many other species, became extinct.

It is hard to believe that human activities could have an effect that

The Gaia Theory

In the 1960s, the National Aeronautics and Space Administration (NASA) asked eminent biophysicist Dr. James Lovelock to help them develop methods to detect life on other planets. In the course of his research, Lovelock came up with the Gaia Theory—the idea that Earth is itself a living organism. This superorganism was named Gaia after the mythological Greek goddess who created life from chaos. In Lovelock's view, each species on Earth is actually part of Gaia, just as cells make up the living bodies of plants and animals.

is comparable to an asteroid impact, but it is true. According to many scientists, including University of Michigan paleontologist Catherine Badgely, there is a mass extinction happening now that has been triggered by human population growth. As humans spread over the planet, wild lands are converted first to farms and then to cities. When land is developed, most of the native plants and animals that live there die or drastically reduce in number.

Habitat loss is one of the greatest threats to endangered species. If their habitats remain unprotected, the world may soon witness the extinction of giant pandas, Asian elephants, marine turtles, and hundreds more species.

*Many animals, including the giant panda, may soon
become extinct due to human activity.*

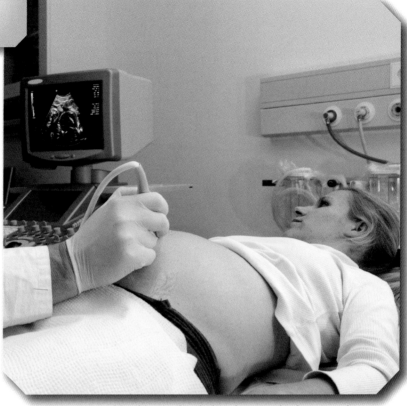

Better prenatal health care has led to decreased infant mortality and has had an impact on birth rates.

THE STATUS OF WOMEN

As demographic transition graphs demonstrate, there is a relationship between industrialization and a decline in birth rates. Experts expected that industrialization was the cause, but, as scientists Paul and Anne Ehrlich and Gretchen Daily explained, one surprising factor turned out to be more important:

> By the end of the 1970s, it had become inescapably clear that "industrialization" alone— building airports, highways, factories, hydroelectric projects, and highrise office blocks— had no effect on birth rates. But improving basic health and nutritional conditions (which led to falling infant mortality rates and rising life expectancies), educating women, and granting them a measure of independence did have direct effects, sometimes dramatic ones.[1]

GORETTI NYABENDA'S STORY

A measure of independence made all the difference for Goretti Nyabenda, a 35-year-old mother of six from Burundi, Africa. In Burundi, it is traditional for husbands to exercise some authority over their wives, but Nyabenda's husband, Bernard, was more authoritarian than most. He beat his wife and would not allow her to leave their small property without him. Although Nyabenda helped support the family by growing vegetables, she was never allowed to handle money. Nyabenda recalled:

> I was wretched. Because I always stayed in the house. I didn't know other people and I was all on my own. My husband said

a wife's job is to cook, stay in the house, or work in the fields. I lived that way, so I was frustrated and angry. [2]

This changed when Nyabenda and her mother-in-law began attending meetings sponsored by the humanitarian organization CARE. This organization revived an ancient African tradition of group banking, in which members pool their money and offer small business loans to members. Nyabenda borrowed two dollars and used it to buy fertilizer that boosted the yield from her potato

A Demographic Mystery

After World War II (1939–1945), well-meaning aid workers began canvassing the developing world, providing vaccinations, information on hygiene and nutrition, and antibiotics to cure infections. They inadvertently created a disaster. Birth rates had evolved over millennia to compensate for high mortality rates, keeping populations stable. When life-saving technologies, but not birth control, were distributed to developing nations, population explosions resulted.

Family planning programs seemed to be the answer. These programs arrived in developing nations in the 1960s, but for several decades, no significant declines in birth rates were seen. Conventional wisdom was that birth rates would naturally decline as development progressed. This had occurred in Western nations predictably enough to generate demographic transition charts, but mysteriously, these charts did not apply everywhere. Through the 1960s and 1970s, uneven progress was seen around the world. Birth rates declined with industrialization in South Korea and Taiwan, but not in Mexico and Brazil. What made the difference? Surprisingly, the crucial factor that slowed birth rates was independence for women.

garden. The $7.50 profit from that harvest allowed her to pay back the loan and start a business making and selling banana beer.

"Now Bernard doesn't bother me. He sees that I can do things, so he asks my opinions. He sees that I can contribute," said Nyabenda.[3]

Although Nyabenda never had a chance to go to school, she is learning to read at CARE meetings. CARE also offers health care for women and children and birth control injections for the women who want them.

"I got injections for family planning, and if I'd known about this earlier, I wouldn't have had six kids. Maybe just three," Nyabenda said. "But if I hadn't been in the group at all, I would have wanted ten kids."[4]

Results of Empowering Women

Successful and independent women are common in the United States, so it may be difficult for an American to understand why empowering women is an issue. Women from the United States have

Microcredit Loans

Microcredit organizations match poor people needing small loans with lenders. Loans are used to start or improve businesses, which help the recipients become self-sufficient. Lenders can browse profiles of loan applicants and choose the individuals they wish to receive their loans. Loan amounts can be as little as $25 or as large as several thousand dollars.

more freedom than women in most other countries. In much of the world, women are expected to obey their husbands and fathers. Especially in male-dominated regions of the Middle East, Africa, and South Asia, women may not have the same rights as men. Depending on the nation, women might not be allowed to vote, drive a car, or choose their own husbands.

Fathers Selling Daughters

In Asia, it is not unusual for poor fathers to sell their own children to pay debts or feed their starving families. In May of 2008, Rabia, an 11-year-old Afghan girl, was sold by her father for $2,000. The father, known as Sayed Ali, later expressed his remorse, saying, "I know people will say I am a cruel and merciless father who sold his own child, but those who say so don't know my hardship and have never felt the hunger that my family suffers."[5]

Young wives in developing nations may have little say in family planning decisions. They defer instead to mothers-in-law and husbands, who often want large families. This is historically true of the Maya of Central America, who consider the number of offspring to be an indicator of a man's virility. As a result, Mayan men—especially the older ones—are likely to oppose the use of birth control. In the Mayan culture, child care is mostly women's work; so extra children do not increase the workload on fathers. It is not uncommon for wives to avoid conflict by secretly visiting clinics

Mayan women have few choices concerning birth control.

for birth control injections. As Ana, a 34-year-old Mayan mother of eight, confided to female health-care workers:

> *My idea is to stay with the number of children I have now, but my husband doesn't want us to use birth control . . . it's a sign that I don't love him. But that is a lie, I just want to space the children to have more materially for them . . . But I am secretly doing something—getting injections. I hope that I will not get pregnant during the next two years while my youngest baby is growing.*[6]

LITERACY AND BIRTH RATES

In most of the world, a son's education takes priority over that of a daughter's. As a result, two-thirds of the world's 900 million illiterate adults are women. Birth rates drop when women learn to read, but why? A great deal of information about birth control is circulated through print. Educated women know that when their bodies have time to recuperate between pregnancies, their health and the health of their babies improves. Additionally, girls who finish school understand the importance of clean water and good nutrition, so their babies are more likely to survive. Parents who are confident that their infants will survive tend to have fewer children.

Literacy opens doors to the job market, giving employed wives a boost in status at home. As a result of their income, women gain clout in family planning negotiations. Husbands come to appreciate and depend upon their wives' incomes—incomes that would be threatened without birth control.

Unequal Rights in the United States

Although American women are some of the most fortunate in the world, they earn only 77¢ for every dollar men earn. Part of the reason is that women choose lower paying jobs, such as teaching or nursing. However, even when women perform the same jobs as men, they earn less.

Education empowers women to make informed choices in their lives.

China's one-child policy regulates population growth in the country.

GOVERNMENTAL REGULATIONS

*S*ome governments try to regulate populations by enacting policies that either encourage or discourage childbearing. Worldwide, populations are skyrocketing, but populations in some countries are shrinking. Each nation makes decisions that are in its own best interest, often without considering what is best for the planet as a whole.

China is a country that stands out for its efforts to combat rapid population growth. On the other side of the equation are shrinking or stable countries such as Japan and France, whose governments are encouraging women to have more children.

GOVERNMENTS ENCOURAGING POPULATION GROWTH

There are two reasons nations may want large populations: money and power. Regarding money, corporations dislike shrinking populations because every person is a consumer. Large populations mean many customers and potentially larger profits. Governments share that concern, and they have several others to add.

Stable or Declining Populations

The 20 countries with stable or declining populations in order of the highest to lowest rate of decrease include:
- Ukraine
- Russia
- Belarus
- Bulgaria
- Latvia
- Lithuania
- Hungary
- Romania
- Estonia
- Moldova
- Croatia
- Germany
- Czech Republic
- Japan
- Poland
- Slovakia
- Austria
- Italy
- Slovenia
- Greece

Gross Domestic Product

The gross domestic product (GDP) represents the total value of all the goods and services produced in a nation in a year. It is a measure of the size of the economy. One goal of capitalism is to keep the economy growing, since stagnant economies are at risk of collapse. A growing economy means more production, more jobs, and more money for investors. The problem with this system is that economies cannot grow indefinitely on finite planetary resources.

Governments of shrinking nations are worried about the support of their senior citizens. This is because most nations levy taxes to pay for medical care and pensions for elders. A declining population naturally has more old people than young ones, placing an extra tax burden on young people. Working parents are doubly stressed since they are responsible for elders as well as their own children.

On the issue of power, governments may want large populations for two reasons. First, large populations enable nations to field massive armies and, even in peacetime, military power translates into international influence. Second, large populations mean large economies. Nations with large economies are influential because they are important trading partners with other countries.

WHY POPULATIONS SHRINK

Between now and the year 2050, it is predicted that Ukraine's population will decline by 43 percent, Russia's will lose 22 percent, and Italy's will be down by 12 percent. Some losses may be offset by immigration, as is happening in the United States. Currently, 20 countries have populations that are either stable or declining. Most are in Europe, and only one—Japan—is in Asia. In the absence of war, famine, or other disasters, what social and economic factors cause populations to decline? The situation in Japan provides one possible answer.

Japan has the third-largest economy in the world, but it has been in a recession since 2008. Workers there are on edge, fearful of losing their jobs. After every wave of layoffs, the workload on remaining employees increases. Office workers typically stay at their desks late into the evening. Hard work is so engrained in the culture that the Japanese language has a word for working to death: *karoshi*.

This lifestyle makes parenting difficult, especially for working mothers. Cultures change slowly, so men typically expect working wives to perform most of the housework and child care at home. Day care and school tuition are expensive as well. So many

*Japan's aging population and low birth numbers
have led to a population decline.*

Japanese families have only one child. In 2009, the
number of births in Japan fell below the number of
deaths, resulting in a population decline of almost
46,000 people.

"Uncertainty over the economy and employment
has lowered people's motivation for marriage and
having children more than expected," says Shigeki
Matsuda, senior director at the Dai-Ichi Life
Research Institute in Tokyo.[1]

The Japanese government is taking measures to
reverse the population decline. New parents will
receive monthly payments totaling the equivalent

of US$3,300 every year for each child from birth through age 15. In 2010, the government also began picking up the bill for school tuition, an expense formerly paid by parents.

These steps may boost birth rates slightly, but they tend to be less effective than governments hope. Without Japanese husbands pitching in on housework and corporations offering family-friendly policies, "All the money in the world may not make a long-term difference," says David Coleman, a professor of demography at Oxford University.[2]

CHINA'S ONE-CHILD POLICY

The other extreme is China, which enacted a one-child policy in 1979 to control overpopulation. The one-child policy was established for good reason. The overpopulation problem in China was, and still is, severe. Pollution, freshwater shortages, and the loss of farmland threaten the health of residents. Since the establishment of population controls, life expectancy has risen from 65 in 1980 to 75 in 2010.

Despite its success, China's one-child policy is widely criticized because of the severe tactics once used to enforce it. Human rights abuses unquestionably took place, especially when forced abortions were used to terminate unauthorized pregnancies. Public pressure, including a few violent uprisings, eliminated the forced-abortion rule. Forced abortions are now illegal.

Instead, cash bonuses are awarded to citizens who undergo surgical sterilization and to couples who reach age 60 with only a single child or two daughters. Fines of up to $65,000 are levied against violators who have extra children, but

Environmental Degradation in China

"China has gone through an industrialization in the past twenty years that many developing countries needed one hundred years to complete," said Pan Yue, vice minister of China's Ministry of Environmental Protection.[3]

This industrialization has had a steep environmental price. Freshwater supplies are scarce, and lax pollution laws have allowed factories to contaminate much of what remains. China's Council on Foreign Relations estimates that 200 million tons (181 million metric tons) of untreated sewage and industrial pollutants are dumped into waterways each year. On land, abundant herds of livestock graze 5,800 square miles (15,000 sq km) of grasslands into deserts annually. The air in large cities is so polluted that people can barely see across streets through the haze. China also leads the world in greenhouse gas emissions.

In China, emissions from burning coal contribute to 400,000 deaths each year. Burning coal also harms the environment by causing acid rain. Acid rain is created when sulfur in coal smoke reacts with oxygen in the air to form sulfuric acid. Sulfuric acid is a major component of acid rain, which kills trees, fish, and amphibians. Acid rain also dissolves marble, doing irreparable damage to historic statues and architecture.

wealthy families often pay the fines gladly. As one affluent businessman said, "I have plenty of money, and if I want to spend that money on having more children I can afford to."[4]

China's one-child rule has since been modified to allow an extra child for rural farm families and for couples whose first baby was a daughter. The reason that the rules have exceptions around daughters is that in China, as in many Asian nations, sons are preferred over daughters. The preference is not only due to discrimination, although that is a major factor. Parents feel more secure about their old age if they have a male child. Boys traditionally care for their own elderly parents, while girls take care of their in-laws. The one-child rule is changing this custom.

Since 1986, ultrasound technology has enabled Chinese couples to discover the sex of their

Urban Daughters

Chinese city dwellers with single daughters have begun showering girls with the kinds of benefits once reserved for boys. The economic boom makes funds available for doting parents to spend on music and language lessons, good schools, and top-quality health care for their daughters. Rural girls are still overlooked in favor of their brothers, but discrimination there appears to be declining as well.

fetus before birth. This has led to the selective abortion of female fetuses, despite laws banning the practice. A study from the *British Medical Journal* determined that China's skewed gender ratios are almost entirely due to sex-selective abortion. There are now 32 million more Chinese males than females under age 20, leaving many men unable to marry. This is an unprecedented social experiment, and the world is watching to see what will happen. One thing is already clear: Chinese women now have their pick of husbands.

China has taken steps to control its population, but growth is still occurring around the world. As populations grow, more resources are needed for humans to survive.

Child Abductions in China

Child abductions are on the rise throughout China. Criminal gangs abduct baby boys and then sell them to couples desperate for a son. Couples may pay up to US$6,000 for a baby boy. Poor farmers and migrant workers are usually targeted for these abductions.

To even out the gender imbalance due to male child preference, people in Shanghai, China, are now having more female children.

Chapter 8

Oil field pump jacks extract oil from underground reserves.

DECLINING RESOURCES

Rising human populations are on a collision course with declining resources. The resources include all the things people depend on for survival, such as fertile soil, clean water, wild fish, forests, and fossil fuels.

A Cree Indian proverb poetically states the result of living out of balance with nature:

> *Only when the last tree has been cut down, only when the last river has been poisoned, only when the last fish has been caught, only then will you find that money cannot be eaten.* [1]

Many resources are being depleted, but the decline of oil is perhaps the greatest concern. This is because accessible oil reserves are declining, and untapped supplies are in land under deep water or in other difficult-to-reach places. There will still be oil in 100 years, but reaching it will probably be too costly to be profitable.

Eating Oil?

Glancing around any ordinary home in the United States, it is easy to see that the occupants are dependent on fossil fuels for heating, cooling, refrigeration, and electricity. However, one use of oil may be difficult to spot: its importance to food production. Conventional farming is heavily reliant on oil. Large farm equipment runs on diesel fuel, and fossil fuels are used to synthesize nitrogen fertilizers, pesticides, and herbicides. Irrigation pumps, crop storage, transport, and refrigeration all use energy—most of which comes from oil, coal, and natural gas.

In a 2002 study at the Johns Hopkins Bloomberg School of Public Health, researchers calculated that developed nations use three calories of fossil fuels for every calorie of food produced. Transport and packaging costs bring the fuel total up to a seven to ten calorie investment. These figures are averages because energy inputs differ depending on the food and the distance it is transported. Beef calls for one of the highest energy

Water Problems

Freshwater supplies are decreasing due to a combination of factors including deforestation, climate change, overuse, and pollution. Much of the world's crops are grown on irrigated land, but not all irrigation water comes from rivers. Much of it is pumped out of underground deposits of water called aquifers.

Irrigating with groundwater may cause problems if the water has high concentrations of dissolved salts. Salts may accumulate in the soil until no crops can grow. Some farms in the western parts of the United States were irrigated for years with well water, leaving white crusts of salt in patches on the ground. One solution is to catch rainwater, which has few dissolved minerals. When rainwater is used for irrigation, it flushes salts deeper into the earth, below root level.

Another concern with groundwater is that aquifers are being depleted faster than they are regenerated. This is bad news for residents of Texas, Oklahoma, and Kansas, where wells are already running dry. Many farmers there have turned to dryland farming, which is dependent only upon rainfall. Yields from dryland farming are much lower than those from irrigated farms. Both groundwater depletion and salt buildup are signs of overshoot because they reduce food supplies.

investments, at 35 calories of fuel per calorie of meat produced.

"This energy deficit can only be maintained because of the availability of cheap fossil fuels, a temporary gift from the Earth's geologic past," said American journalist and author Richard Heinberg.[2]

The predicament is that fossil-fuel supplies are temporary. Barring an unprecedented increase in renewable energy use, the decline of oil will almost certainly result in global food shortages.

Malnourishment

The World Health Organization estimates that 30 percent of the world population is malnourished, meaning that they do not get enough calories, protein, vitamins, or minerals. Malnourished people are not always thin. Malnourished people can also be overweight from a high-calorie, vitamin-poor diet of processed foods.

Overshoot

Fossil fuels have artificially increased the carrying capacity of the planet, at least for the short-term. When a population temporarily exceeds its carrying capacity, the phenomenon is called an overshoot. No population—animal or human—can stay above its carrying capacity indefinitely, so overshoots do not last long. Among wild animals, overshoots are followed by equally steep declines. After a decline, the carrying capacity is virtually always lower than it was before. This is because overshoots damage the land, reducing the number of organisms that can be sustainably supported.

Imagine a population of rabbits that eat vegetation and reproduce rapidly. If rabbits become too numerous, they graze until there is no more vegetation, and then they starve. After most of the rabbits are gone, it takes time for the vegetation to grow back. If some plants have died out entirely, those species may never return. The carrying capacity has been reduced.

Overshoot

The moment a species overshoots its carrying capacity, no catastrophe or sudden die-off heralds the event. Populations may still increase in the short-term, but a decline is in the future. Over-populated animals die from disease, predation, parasitism, and starva-tion, but humans may be clever enough to avoid those fates. People can choose to control their populations gradually, preventing disastrous die-offs.

In human terms, the story is similar. Heavy use of chemicals temporarily increases crop yields, but it damages the soil structure and kills normal soil organisms. Over time, pests evolve a resistance to poisons, and the land is damaged by erosion and the loss of organic matter. Degraded lands begin to decline in productivity, and marginal lands turn to desert. Arable land is paved for development, game animals die off, and wastes accumulate, so food production declines. This is an overshoot, and this is happening right now.

The key difference between populations of people and populations of animals is human intellect. Rabbits will reproduce until they starve, but people have other choices. As David Pimentel, professor of ecology and agricultural science at Cornell University, put it, "If humans do not control their numbers, nature will."[3]

PEAK OIL

Most experts agree that world oil production peaked in 2010. This means that oil production will gradually decline over the next century at roughly the same rate that it increased between 1910 and 2010. The situation is problematic because world population is almost double what it was 40 years ago. If current growth rates continue, the world population will increase by 2.8 billion within 50 years. Demand for oil is increasing as developing nations aspire to match the consumptive

Will Climate Change Cause War?

In 2007, the UN Security Council held its first formal discussion about the potential of climate change to provoke wars. Climate change may cause altered rainfall patterns, rising sea levels, and declines in food production, all of which would intensify competition for resources. In advance of the 2010 UN climate talks, British scientists warned that rising sea levels could displace up to 1 billion people this century, sparking territorial conflicts.

lifestyles of the West. These factors will combine to drive oil and gas prices up.

More critically, oil is being used to maintain the human population above carrying capacity, so as oil declines, food prices will increase. Renewable energies from solar, wind, and geothermal sources will be essential, but they may not be available quickly enough. In 2009, only 10 percent of electricity production in the United States came from renewable energy.

Peak Oil

Shell Oil Company geologist Dr. Marion King Hubbert was the first to discover that oil production rises and falls in a bell-shaped curve. Hubbert correctly predicted the peak of US oil production, which occurred from 1970 to 1971.

These facts have geologist and petroleum industry executive Colin Campbell deeply concerned. When asked about the likely effects of hitting the downslope of oil production, Campbell did not mince words:

Simply stated: war, starvation, economic recession, possibly even the extinction of [humans], insofar as the evolution of life on earth has always been accomplished by the extinction of over-adapted species . . . leaving simpler forms to continue, and eventually giving

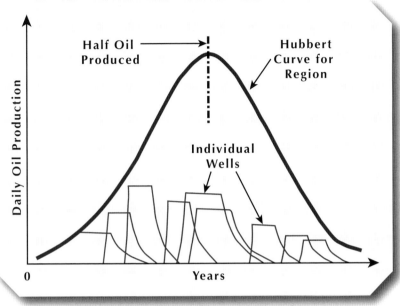

*The Hubbert Curve chart shows how oil production
will reach a peak before it falls.*

rise [to] new more adapted species. If [the human race]
figures out how to move back to simplicity, he will be the first
[species ever] to do so.[4]

Not everyone shares Campbell's gloomy outlook.
Many people see a bright future for humanity,
one in which creativity and innovation will solve
today's problems. Technology came to the rescue
once before, in the 1960s, when the population
approached carrying capacity and starvation became
a major problem.

The Green Revolution, with its pesticides, high-yield crops, and petroleum-derived fertilizers, allowed humans to reach population densities never before seen on Earth. As Earth's population increases, even more food will need to be produced. Another Green Revolution is in the works, this time offering controversial genetically modified crops. ⌐

Alternative energy sources, such as solar and wind power, will need to be increasingly used as fossil fuels are depleted.

Finding ways to use less resources, such as using water bottle refilling stations, will reduce the effects of overpopulation.

SOLUTIONS FOR A SUSTAINABLE WORLD

fter considering the factors that limit population growth, it is clear that future population levels cannot be predicted by simply calculating reproductive rates over time. After all, the world does not have an infinite food supply.

Resource depletion, pollution, and industrialization present additional limits to population growth. These limiting factors must be considered for any population prediction to be meaningful.

A COMPUTER SIMULATION'S WARNING

In the early 1970s, an international think tank called the Club of Rome commissioned scientists Donella H. Meadows, Dennis L. Meadows, Jørgen Randers, and William W. Behrens III to develop a model of world population that considered both reproductive rates and limiting factors. The results were a computer simulation called World3 and a controversial book entitled *Limits to Growth (LTG)*. The book encountered opposition from business interests because of its premise that economic and population growth cannot continue indefinitely.

In 1991, three *LTG* authors (Meadows, Meadows, and Randers) revisited World3 to provide the program with updated data. "We were afraid that we would no longer be able to find in the model any possibility of a believable, sufficient,

The State of the World

The World3 computer model shows a scenario that will probably occur if current trends continue. The population decline does not have to be a result of violence or starvation. If humanity makes the right choices, it could be a peaceful shift toward living in balance with the planet.

sustainable future for all the world's people," wrote the team.[1] The results of the updated simulation turned out to be sobering, but not hopeless.

If current trends continue, World3 predicts that the population will increase until about 2030. At that point, resource depletion, pollution, and food shortages will increase the death rate and bring about a decline. As the population declines, pollution declines as well, indicating some degree of ecosystem recovery.

The authors emphasized:

This decline is not inevitable. To avoid it two changes are necessary. The first is a comprehensive revision of policies and practices that perpetuate growth in material consumption and in population. The second is a rapid, drastic increase in the efficiency with which materials and energy are used.[2]

For these changes to be implemented, society has to make more than physical changes. Cultural shifts will need to occur as well. Land bases must become more important

Status Symbols

Hundreds of years ago, most people lived in small villages. Individuals earned status by using their skills to benefit their communities. Now that modern cities have developed, residents no longer know all their neighbors. People advertise their social status to strangers with symbols such as flashy cars, fancy clothes, and jewelry. This material culture has its roots in a normal human desire to be appreciated.

Vehicles using renewable power sources, such as this solar scooter made by Chinese students, will become even more important in the future.

than products and healthy ecosystems valued more highly than profits. If these changes seem unlikely, then a decline may well be on the way. A gradual decline in population would benefit people and the environment, but no one wants to see a sudden collapse. Catastrophic population declines are usually associated with war, famine, and epidemics of infectious disease.

Road Map to Sustainability

"We are living today at the end of the period of greatest material abundance in human history," says Richard Heinberg, author and senior fellow-in-residence at the Post Carbon Institute.[3]

Adjusting to the end of fossil-fueled material abundance may be a daunting prospect, but this process must begin now. Civilization's infrastructure is made of interrelated systems for transportation, communication, food production, and power generation. All of these were designed to run on fossil fuels, so they will all need remodeling. The process of bringing renewable energy online will itself cost energy, so it must begin while oil is plentiful. It will take an international government-coordinated effort to bring about such sweeping changes.

The most essential step toward sustainability is to control runaway

You Can Help

You can influence your parents' buying decisions. You can use that power to create a more sustainable future. To be environmentally conscious, encourage your family to buy "green" products such as hybrid cars, solar hot water heaters, and sustainably grown food. Organic food is usually more expensive than conventionally grown food, but your family may find that conserving energy saves enough to pay for organic groceries.

population growth. No amount of recycling or energy conservation can save the planet if exponential population growth continues. Assuming that the global community can get a grip on this problem, what might an optimal population be? Too few people might mean that civilization would make little progress on technological and cultural pursuits. Pushing the population to the planet's limits would necessitate driving other species to extinction, as is happening now. How many people can live sustainably on Earth? The answer can only be projected—no one knows.

Conservation efforts now will mean fewer species are extinguished, fewer forests leveled, and fewer fish stocks decimated. After the population finally does decline, as it almost certainly will, more of those treasures will be left alive for future generations to appreciate.

The capitalist economic system does not need to be abandoned, just modified. This economy based on endless growth must be replaced by a system based on sustainability. Business ventures such as clear-cutting forests, mountaintop removal mining, and damming rivers are profitable, but they all convert living ecosystems into dead products.

When the products are sold, only a few entrepreneurs benefit. The rest of the world is left ecologically impoverished.

There is a lot of healing to be done. Heinberg said:

> *Even if we cease all environmentally destructive practices tomorrow, we still face the momentum of processes already set in motion throughout decades of deforestation, overfishing, topsoil erosion, and fossil-fuel combustion. First and foremost of these processes is, of course, global climate change, which will almost certainly have serious impacts on world agriculture even if future carbon emissions decline sharply and soon.* [4]

WHAT INDIVIDUALS CAN DO

No one person can stop exponential population growth or global industrialization, but individuals can help prepare their communities for the changes that are

Peak Oil Anxiety

It is normal for people to experience anxiety when they come to terms with the reality of peak oil. Although anxiety is unsettling, it can also motivate citizens to make positive changes. People of all ages can attend political meetings, become environmental activists, or work to reduce their household energy use. Civilization is about to undergo an overhaul, but this does not mean that civilization is coming to an end.

to come. Today's adults will probably not live to see the full impact of the resource decline, but they can help younger generations prepare. Interested people can gather into community groups and plan for the future.

Supplies of food, water, and fuel may become increasingly local as oil prices rise. This does not mean that people will starve, but it means that locally grown fresh produce will likely replace trucked-in processed food. Community gardens and greenhouses may become essential because they build social ties as they

Transition Town

Transition Town is an international organization whose mission is to facilitate a peaceful, abundant transition to a post-fossil-fuel economy. Local branches of this organization are appearing in many communities, where they meet together, eat together, and plan for a sustainable future. Transition Town members are not "doom and gloom" environmentalists. In fact, they have a surprisingly cheerful outlook about the process of energy descent.

As Transition Town members from Southend-on-Sea, in the United Kingdom, say:

Climate change and Peak oil can cause us to feel confronted by something overwhelmingly huge that we cannot do anything about. The central message of the Transition Movement is that this state of mind is not the place to start from if we want to achieve something, do something or create something. Indeed, by shifting our mind-set we can actually recognize the coming post-cheap oil era as an opportunity rather than a threat, and design the future low carbon age to be thriving, resilient and abundant—somewhere much better to live than our current alienated consumer culture based on greed, war and the myth of perpetual growth.[5]

provide food. Most water pumps run on electricity, making water supplies susceptible to power outages. Solar panels and home wind generators could take up the slack if the electric blackouts become common.

The next century holds many challenges, but there are choices to be made that can affect the issue of overpopulation. Women can make choices about the size of their families. Citizens can decide to reduce their effect on the environment by reducing waste, reusing materials, and being more energy efficient. Governments can make choices about how their countries use and treat natural resources. Nature will find a way to equalize itself. Humans have the choice every day to help nature find its balance.

*Community gardens, where people can grow their own food,
may become a vital necessity in the future.*

TIMELINE

2–5 million years ago	200,000 years ago	50,000–100,000 years ago
Early humans struggle to survive on Earth.	A bottleneck extinguishes all but one human lineage.	A second bottleneck occurs, possibly due to a volcanic eruption on the Indonesian island of Sumatra.

540–590	1347–1352	ca. 1770
The Plague of Justinian kills half of Europe's population.	The Black Plague kills one-third of Europe's population.	The Industrial Revolution in Europe brings a population explosion.

14,000 years ago	4500 BCE	476–1453 CE

Permanent settlements are established in the Middle East, marking the movement from a nomadic to a settled lifestyle.

As the Neolithic Revolution spreads, farming begins in the British Isles.

Hygiene problems in medieval towns increase the risk of disease and limit population growth.

1803	1845	1945–1960s

Thomas Robert Malthus writes his population essay.

The General Enclosure Act forces English peasants off their land and into urban areas.

Vaccinations, medicine, and health education are brought to developing nations, causing a population spike.

TIMELINE

1960s

Famines mark local overshoots of human population.

1960s

The Green Revolution begins. This increases global crop yields, leading to overpopulation.

1970–1971

US oil production peaks.

1991

The World3 computer simulation warns of population decline after the year 2030.

2002

The United Nations creates three population projections for the year 2050.

1979

China enacts its
one-child policy.

1980–1983

An ozone hole
develops over the
South Pole.

2010

The global life
expectancy reaches
a record 68.9 years.

2010

HIV/ AIDS
reduces African
life expectancy
by 11 years.

2010

The world's oil
production peaks.

ESSENTIAL FACTS

AT ISSUE

❖ Overpopulation occurred when populations grew too big for their resource base.

❖ The Neolithic Revolution was the transition from a hunter-gatherer lifestyle to farming. The new settled lifestyle triggered an increase in population.

❖ Disease has been one of the most important limiting factors on human populations. As crowding increased, the risk of disease increased as well.

❖ The population curve began spiking during the Industrial Revolution in Europe.

❖ In the 1960s and 1970s, famines motivated agricultural scientists to develop more productive crop varieties. The resulting Green Revolution increased harvests but worsened overpopulation.

❖ Polar ice caps are melting, and sea levels could rise enough to threaten coastal communities. Global warming is thought to be caused by greenhouse gases, which are gases that trap heat in the atmosphere. Carbon dioxide is a key greenhouse gas, and it comes mostly from the combustion of fossil fuels.

❖ Birth rates decline as literacy rises and as women gain equality with men. Improvements in literacy also reduce infant mortality rates.

CRITICAL DATES

4500 BCE

Farming began in the British Isles.

540 CE

The first epidemic to devastate Europe, the Plague of Justinian, killed half the population of Europe.

1347–1352

The Black Plague killed one-third of Europe's population.

ca. 1770

The Industrial Revolution in Europe caused a population explosion.

1960s

Famines marked local overshoots of human population. The Green Revolution began, which increased global crop yields and has led to overpopulation.

2010

The global life expectancy reached a record 68.9 years.

QUOTES

"The world's forests need to be seen for what they are: giant global utilities, providing essential services to humanity on a vast scale. Rainforests store carbon, which is lost to the atmosphere when they burn, increasing global warming. The life they support cleans the atmosphere of pollutants and feeds it with moisture. They help regulate our climate and sustain the lives of some of the poorest people on this Earth."—*Charles, the Prince of Wales*

"Through the animal and vegetable kingdoms, nature has scattered the seeds of life abroad with the most profuse and liberal hand. She has been comparatively sparing in the room, and the nourishment necessary to rear them . . . The race of plants, and race of animals shrink under this great restrictive law. And the race of man cannot, by any efforts of reason, escape from it. Among plants and animals its effects are waste of seed, sickness, and premature death. Among mankind, misery and vice."—*Thomas Malthus, British scholar*

Glossary

arable
Land that is suitable for farming.

benevolent
Intending good toward others.

controversial
Debatable; a point of dispute.

degradation
The process by which land loses health and productivity.

ecosystem
A group of living things interacting with each other and the environment.

ecosystem services
Important benefits to humans that arise from functioning ecosystems, such as purification of water and production of oxygen.

exacerbated
Worsened; made more severe.

exploitation
To make use of meanly or unfairly for one's own advantage.

extrapolated
Data or experience projected, extended, or expanded into an area not known or experienced.

hypothetical
Based on a suggested idea or theory; imagined as an example.

indigenous
People who are native to a particular region or environment.

innovation
A new idea, device, or method.

languishing
> To continue for a long time, without activity or progress, in an unpleasant or unwanted situation.

literacy
> The ability to read and write.

overshoot
> The situation of population growth beyond carrying capacity.

populous
> Having a large population.

recession
> A period of time in which there is a decrease in economic activity and many people do not have jobs.

repercussion
> Negative consequences for an action.

retribution
> Punishment for doing something wrong.

rife
> Very common and often unpleasant.

transpiration
> The process by which water moves in through plant roots, rises up through the plant or tree, and evaporates from leaves.

ADDITIONAL RESOURCES

SELECTED BIBLIOGRAPHY

Ehrlich, Paul R., Anne H. Ehrlich, and Gretchen C. Daily. *The Stork and the Plow*. New Haven, CT: G.P. Putnam's Sons, 1995. Print.

Kristof, Nicholas D., and Sheryl WuDunn. *Half the Sky*. New York: Random, 2009. Print.

Moffett, George D. *Critical Masses*. New York: Penguin, 1994. Print.

Russell, Lester. *Plan B: Rescuing a Planet Under Stress and a Civilization in Trouble*. Norton, 2003. Print.

United Nations. *World Population to 2300*. New York: United Nations, 2004. Web. 1 Dec. 2010.

FURTHER READINGS

Hopkins, Rob. *The Transition Handbook: From Oil Dependency to Local Resilience*. White River Junction, VT: Chelsea Green, 2008. Print.

Zeaman, John. *Overpopulation*. New York: Franklin Watts, 2001. Print.

WEB LINKS

To learn more about world population, visit ABDO Publishing Company online at **www.abdopublishing.com**. Web sites about world population are featured on our Book Links page. These links are routinely monitored and updated to provide the most current information available.

For More Information

For more information on this subject, contact or visit the following organizations:

The Central Rocky Mountain Permaculture Institute
2001 East Cedar Drive
Basalt, CO 81621
970-927-4158
www.crmpi.org
CRMPI provides a living demonstration of abundant sustainable living. Weekly tours are given by Jerome Osentowski, the founder and director of CRMPI. The tours detail the forest garden and greenhouses. A half-day workshop is also available.

EcoTarium Museum
222 Harrington Way
Worcester, MA 01604
508-929-2700
www.ecotarium.org
This is an indoor-outdoor museum, with animals, a planetarium, exhibits, and nature trails. The *Thinking Globally, Abiding Locally* permanent exhibit focuses on energy use and the effects overuse has on our environment and examines conservation technology.

Monterey Bay Aquarium
886 Cannery Row
Monterey, CA 93940
831-648-4800
www.montereybayaquarium.org
This aquarium has the *Hot Pink Flamingos: Stories of Hope in a Changing Sea* exhibit, that tells the story of climate change through the eyes of ocean animals. It also shows the efforts of people to reduce carbon emissions.

Source Notes

Chapter 1. A Child in a Crowded World

1. *Your Right to Food: Sandeep's Story*. Perf. Sandeep. World Vision Stir, 2010, Film.

2. Graham Paterson. "Alan Greenspan claims Iraq war was really for oil." *timesonline.co.uk*. Sunday Times, 16 Sept. 2007. Web. 3 Dec. 2010.

Chapter 2. The Struggle to Survive

1. Nayan Chanda. "We Are All Africans." *yaleglobal.yale.edu*. Yale Global Online, 21 July 2009. Web. 3 Dec. 2010.

2. David Whitehouse. "Humans came 'close to extinction.'" *BBC Online*. BBC News, 8 Sept. 1998. Web. 3 Dec. 2010.

3. "Thomas Hobbes." *Answers.com*. Answers.com, 2010. Web. 3 Dec. 2010.

4. Jarred Diamond. *Guns, Germs, and Steel*. New York: Norton, 1997. Print. 18.

5. Ibid.

Chapter 3. Influences on Populations

1. "The Black Death, 1348." *EyeWitness to History*. EyeWitness to History, 2001. Web. 3 Dec. 2010.

2. Peter Landry. "Malthus' Essay On Population, Part 3 to the Life & Works of Thomas Robert Malthus." *Biographies*. Biographies, 2010. Web. 3 Dec. 2010.

3. Ibid.

Chapter 4. Predicting the Future

1. George D. Moffett. *Critical Masses*. New York: Penguin, Ltd., 1994. Print. 7.

2. Ibid.

Chapter 5. Ecosystem Services
1. "Rain halts search for Guatemala mudslide victims." *BBC News*. BBC News, 9 June 2010. Web. 3 Dec. 2010.
2. "Prince Charles Quotes." *woopidoo.com*. Woopidoo Quotations, n.d. Web. 3 Dec. 2010.

Chapter 6. The Status of Women
1. Paul R. Ehrlich, Anne H. Ehrlich, and Gretchen C. Daily. *The Stork and the Plow*. New Haven, CT: G.P. Putnam's Sons, 1995. Print. 69.
2. Nicholas D. Kristof and Sheryl WuDunn. *Half the Sky*. New York: Random, 2009. Print. 199–203.
3. Ibid.
4. Ibid.
5. "Afghanistan: 'I sold my daughter to feed the rest of my family.'" *irinnews.org*. Irin Asia, 18 May 2008. Web. 3 Dec. 2010.
6. Miriam Salvador and Adrienne Wiebe. "Three Generations of Mayan Women's Perspectives on Reproductive Health." *www.cahr.uvic.ca*. Centre for Aboriginal Health Research, 2008. Web. 3 Dec. 2010.

Chapter 7. Governmental Regulations
1. Ian Rowley. "Anxious Japanese Are Working Themselves to Death." *Bloomberg Businessweek*. Businessweek, 6 Sept. 2009. Web. 3 Dec. 2010.
2. Daisuke Wakabayashi and Miho Inada. "Baby Bundle: Japan's Cash Incentive for Parenthood." *online.wsj.com*. Wall Street Journal. 10 Sept. 2009. Web. 3 Dec. 2010.
3. Carin Zissis. "China's Environmental Crisis." *cfr.org*. Council on Foreign Relations. 2008. Web. 3 Dec. 2010.
4. Jeffrey Hays. "One-child Policy in China." *factsanddetails.com*. Facts and Details. 4 Jan. 2010. Web. 3 Dec. 2010.

SOURCE NOTES CONTINUED

Chapter 8. Declining Resources

1. "Cree Indian Prophecy." *Iwise Wisdom on Demand*. Iwise Wisdom on Demand, n.d. Web. 3 Dec. 2010.

2. Tracy Salisbury and Brenda Frick. "Agriculture in the Age of Declining Fossil Fuels." *oacc.info*. Organic Agriculture Centre of Canada, 12 Jan. 2008. Web. 3 Dec. 2010.

3. David Pimentel and Marcia Pimentel. "The Real Perils of Human Population Growth." *secularhumanism.org*. Council for Secular Humanism, n.d. Web. 3 Dec. 2010.

4. Michael Ruppert. "Colin Campbell on Oil." *fromthewilderness.com*. From the Wilderness Publications, 2002. Web. 3 Dec. 2010.

Chapter 9. Solutions for a Sustainable World

1. Dennis Meadows, Donella Meadows, and Jorgen Randers. "Beyond The Limits To Growth." *context.org*. In Context, 1992. Web. 3 Dec. 2010.

2. Ibid.

3. Richard Heinberg. "Beyond the Limits to Growth." *The Post Carbon Institute*. The Post Carbon Institute, 2010. Web. 3 Dec. 2010.

4. Ibid.

5. "Southend in Transition—Life After Oil." *Southend in Transition*. Southend in Transition, n.d. Web. 11 Jan. 2011.

Index

Index Continued

About the Author

Courtney Farrell is a full-time writer and the author of 13 books for young people. She is interested in wildlife conservation, social justice, and sustainability issues. She lives with her husband and teenaged sons on a ranch in the Colorado mountains.

Photo Credits

Bikas Das/AP Images, cover, 3; Kevin Frayer/AP Images, 6; Ajit Solanki/AP Images, 9; Liu xionbiao/AP Images, 13; Kike Calvo/AP Images, 14, 53, 96, 99 (top); Jerome Delay/AP Images, 19; SSPL/Getty Images, 25, 30; North Wind/North Wind Picture Archives, 26, 97 (top); Barry Thumma/AP Images, 34; Hulton Archive/Getty Images, 37, 97 (bottom); Dmitry Rukhlenko/Shutterstock Images, 38; Red Line Editorial, Inc., 44, 83; Shutterstock Images, 47; Chen Xiaolan/Color China Photo/AP Images, 48, ; Luo Xiaoyun/Color China Photo/AP Images, 57; iStockphoto, 58; Rodrigo Abd/AP Images, 63; Stevens Frederic/Sipa/AP Images, 65; Wang Zirui/Imaginechina/AP Images, 66; Koji Sasahara/AP Images, 70, 99 (bottom); Dong Hongjing/Imaginechina/AP Images, 75; Larry MacDougal/AP Images, 76, 98; James Steidl/Shutterstock Images, 85; Justin Sullivan/Getty Images, 86; CQWB/Imaginechina/AP Images, 89; AFP/Getty Images, 95